MAY 2022 EDITION

AN ANTHOLOGY OF ARTICLES

BRILLOPEDIA

Copyright © Brillopedia
All Rights Reserved.

This book has been published with all efforts taken to make the material error-free after the consent of the author. However, the author and the publisher do not assume and hereby disclaim any liability to any party for any loss, damage, or disruption caused by errors or omissions, whether such errors or omissions result from negligence, accident, or any other cause.

While every effort has been made to avoid any mistake or omission, this publication is being sold on the condition and understanding that neither the author nor the publishers or printers would be liable in any manner to any person by reason of any mistake or omission in this publication or for any action taken or omitted to be taken or advice rendered or accepted on the basis of this work. For any defect in printing or binding the publishers will be liable only to replace the defective copy by another copy of this work then available.

Contents

Preface

"Start writing, no matter what. The water does not flow until the faucet is turned on".

-Louis L'Amour

This book is a bouquet of articles contributed by students, professors and academicians. Hundreds of students and professors are contributing their work to Brillopedia, we are here to provide ample information about Law and Contemporary issues. Our aim is to provide a platform for today's generation to express their views and ideas on law and contemporary law.

CHAPTER ONE

WITCH-HUNT A CURSE TO WOMENHOOD

Author: Ritik Sinha, B.A.,LL.B from Banaras Hindu University, faculty of law.

Co-author: Rishabh Raj, B.A.,LL.B from Manikchand pahade law college.

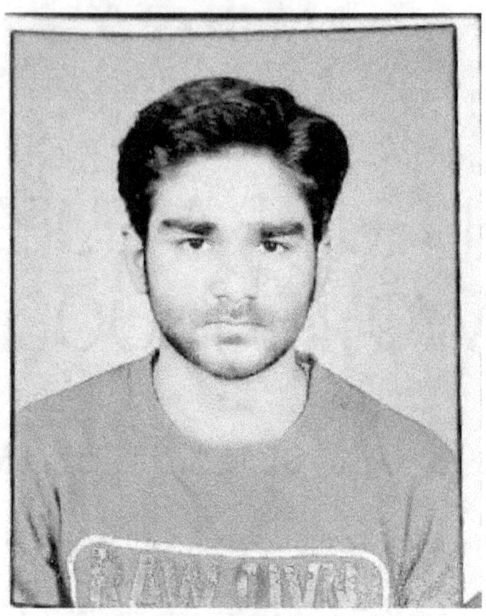

Introduction

We live in the twenty-first century, where our one foot is on Mars and the other on an evil belief. The classical period of witch-hunts in early Modern Europe and Colonial America that took place between year 1450 and 1750. Witch hunting is not new, but between 2000 and 2009, approximately 2500 women died as a result of an allegation of witchcraft and practise of black magic. They were severely beaten and forced to strip off their clothes and were burnt alive. Several cases of accused women being murdered by a mob have been reported. Jharkhand, a state in eastern India, was the site of a recent attack. The victims, all over 60 years old, were pulled from their homes and mercilessly beaten to death with sticks by masked attackers. Numerous cases of witch-hunting have not been reported because the victims were not aware of their existing rights and privileges.

Law in India And World Against Witch Purge

On April 25, 2012, in the case of Mrs. Sashiprava Bindhani vs. Union of India , Witch-hunting, which is common in various states, results in eviction, torture, and murder, but despite the fact that India is a member to CEDAW, no steps have been done to date to enact suitable legislation to address the threat of witch-hunting, which is common in this state. States including as Bihar, Jharkhand, and Chhattisgarh have already made steps to eliminate such practice's, while others have yet to do so. As a result, the petitioner requests that the State be directed to implement legislation in this area.

The National Human Rights Commission (NHRC) has recently requested full reports on witchcraft from Odisha's chief secretary and DGP. The NHRC is concerned about the Odisha's Prevention of Witch-Hunting Act of 2013 implementation and the Odisha Government's devised strategy to stop witch-hunting. According to the NCRB, Odisha has the second greatest number of deaths due to witch-hunting after Jharkhand.i Furthermore, citing NCRB statistics, the Orissa high court stated that more than 2500 people were tortured and killed in witch hunts between 2000 and 2016.ii

According to sources, Odisha has an annual average of 48 sorcery deaths. Because no legislation exists to address the problem of witch-hunting, it is suggested that this Court direct the State

Government to put relevant legislation before the Legislature and, in the interim, establish guidelines to avoid witch-hunting in the state of Orissa.iii

In the case of Gaurav Jain vs. the State, Bihar was the first state to pass a legislature. In this instance, the court ordered that a committee be formed to recommend whether special legislation should be enacted to prohibit hunting. The Prevention of Witch (Daain) Practice Act, 1999 was passed by the Bihar Legislature (Bihar Act 9 of 1999). The legislature of Chhattisgarh has also passed a similar bill.iv

Several states followed suit, enacting legislation despite existing anti-witch hunt legislation. In many isolated places where women are unaware of the law or are unable to enforce it, relatives accuse them of stealing lands, money, or being misled due to illiteracy and false belief, I remember a case where a woman name Chamri Devi would take turns collecting firewood from the jungle neighbouring Baroti, their village in Ranchi district's Namkum block, 15 km from the Jharkhand state secretariat. Her nephew savagely abused her since her nephew's son had been ill for three months and a local Ojha told him that his aunt had performed black magic on his son, after which the boy's father and uncle arranged a terrible trial, and the devi was mercilessly killed when the trial ended.

Jharkhand has been leading cases of the witch hunt because of not proper educated people. Local people kill innocent women by addressing her a witch, rape them, to acquire their property and sometimes it is being used as a tool for vengeance. Lok Sabha passed a bill regarding witch purge

Whoever, accuses, identifies, or defames a woman by stating she is a Daain, Dayan, Daakan, Dakin, Chudail, Bhootni, Bhootdi, Chilavan, Opri, Ranndkadi, Tonahi, Tonaha, Banamati, Chetabadi, Chillangi, Hawa, Evil Eye, Halka, Daini, or any other term or sign suggesting her to be a witch.

- Whoever accuses a woman of practicing witch purge or performing any puja or using mantra or tantra with the intent of harming another person by supernatural means shall be punished with imprisonment for a term of not less than one year but not more than three years, as well as a fine of not less than one thousand rupees but not more than five thousand rupees. Some provisions relating to the bill's criminal penalties.

1. Punishment for labeling a woman as witch
2. Punishment for intimidating a woman for practicing witchcraft
3. Punishment for assaulting or using criminal force practicing against woman.
4. Punishment for torturous or humiliating acts committed under the guise of witchcraft.

<u>PROSECUTION OF OFFENCES</u>

- Notwithstanding anything comprised in the "Code of Criminal Procedure, 1973".
- Under this Act, every offence is cognizable, non-bailable and non-compoundable.
- Any person, who willfully or otherwise, fails to pay the court-ordered fine is subject to imprisonment U/s 64 of the "Indian Penal Code, 1860".
- 16. (1) The victim is entitled to compensation for the fine imposed as a result of an offence under this Act.
- (2) "The reimbursement paid under sub on (1) may not be combined with any other reimbursement or monetary support provided by the government as an immediate relief to the victim, or with the rehabilitation grant payable under section 24".
- 17. The aggrieved party shall be eligible to file an appeal to the next higher court within ninety days after the day on which the concerned court has issued the ruling, subject to the code's restrictions.

<u>Conclusion</u>

Time to awake for the social discrimination based on gender

Society must recognize that witch trials are not only legally wrong but also morally and religiously wrong, and that they are not justifiable in every village. The government should launch an initiative to educate people about witch-hunting as a crime, and that no one has the right to kill someone simply because some tantric or ojhas have labelled her as a black magic practitioner. Women were burned alive in Europe's last witch trial in the 18th century, but in our country today, women are raped, attacked, murdered, and harassed due of accusations of daain. The majority of witch-hunt cases are now dealt with under section 323 of the Indian Penal Code, 1860.

As a result, "harassment of a woman, violence, social exclusion, and loss of rights are tried in the same way as a common assault. In addition, certain provisions of the Indian Penal Code, 1860, such as section 382 'theft after preparation for causing death, hurt, or restraint in order to commit theft,' sections 339—48 'wrongful restraint and confinement,' sections 320—22, 'Causing grievous hurt,' sections 359—69, 'Kidnapping and abduction,' sections 375—376, 'Rape,' sections 499—501 'Defamation' and section 302, 'Murder".v

In the absence of a strict legal framework to address the problem of witch-hunting, the use of these components has led in ad hoc, uncoordinated, and often insensitive responses to the societal scourge of witch-hunting. A national law, on the other hand, would recognize, comprehend, and remedy the specific injuries and wrongs perpetrated against women who are classified as witches and oppressed. As a specific form of continued prejudice and violence against women in India, witch-hunting must be prevented, prohibited, and prosecuted. As a result, a more coordinated and consistent approach to national law will better address the catastrophic impact of witch-hunting on the lives of targeted women throughout India. It would also help civic society and law enforcement organisations to better mobilise in order to fulfil their responsibilities.vi Women are tormented and beaten to death by being labelled as witches in a society where women are adored as the goddess Durga.

Authors' Bio

I am Rishabh Raj currently pursuing BALLB(2021-26) from Manikchand pahade law college. I have keen interest in legal content writing and research. I am having experience of previous publications on different journals. I also have experience of internships under senior advocates and

NGOs where i learnt making case briefs, made causelist, attended live SC hearings, researched on various cases etc. I enjoy using my writing skills as a medium to contribute to the society. And i welcome many more such opportunities in near future.

CHAPTER TWO

CHILD SEXUAL ABUSE AND ITS Effect ON COGNITIVE, EMOTIONAL AND SOCIAL ASPECTS

Author: Vidhi Krishali, IV Year of B.B.A.,LL.B from Symbiosis Law School, Hyderabad [Symbiosis International (Deemed) University, Pune].

Introduction

Child abuse is an all-embracing issue in India, which frequently has immediate harmful impacts on children and the possibility of many lifetime difficulties. Child sexual abuse (CSA), like it is in many areas of the globe today, is a significant and widespread issue in India. Trauma connected with sexual abuse and several emotional and psychological problems that some children and teenagers cannot overcome may also contribute to halted development. When sexual assault remains undetected, and children are not provided with the protection and psychological help they need, they stay silent.

Child sexual abuse (CSA), in conjunction with force or coercion, is defined as an abuse of power and authority leading to the exploitation of children. This entails situations where the older adults or children have sufficient power and strength to obtain sexual satisfaction from those who are developed immature and where consent of the victim results in the absence of conception. Such satisfaction may entail explicit sexual activity or intrusive and inappropriate actions without direct contact.

Case Study

The horrid case of rape of a minor in Kathua shook the entire nation. The 8-year-old girl was violently raped up by eight random men in a Temple. She was allegedly detained and raped for days in the temple, which seems to have been an attempt to expel the rest of the community from the location.

There were 7 or 8 suspects, Sanji Ram, former revenue officer, Deepak Khajuria and Surendra Verma from Special Police, two investigating officials - Tilak Raj, Chief Constable, and Anand Dutta Sub-Inspector, and Parvesh Kumar, a civilian. The accused of rape and killing a child were convicted. On 10 January, the little girl was abducted at a tiny rural temple in Khathua, Jammu district and Kashmir, and reportedly gang rape was taken. On 17 January, the wounded corpse of the little girl was located in the jungle.

Three individuals were condemned to death by the Special Courts. The master perpetrator of this crime was Sanji Ram. The three major defendants, Deepak Khajuria and Parvesh Kumar have been awarded a death punishment and the 3 have received life imprisonment. They were accused with conspiracy, murder, kidnapping, gang rape, destruction of evidence, drugs and common purpose. The other defendants—Anand Dutta, Tilak Raj and Surendra Verma were sentenced to five years in jail and 50 000 fines for destruction of evidence. But Vishal Jangotra, son of Sanji Ram, was acquitted by the courtroom for 'Benefit of Doubt.' One accused was underage and the examination procedure resumed

There is a coherent demand of "The Protection of Children from Sexual Offences Act" POSCO act in India. But after this act has been performed, instances involving sexual offences against minors are increasing and the penalty mentioned in it is far smaller for the extent of the crime. The legislation should be strictly applied to defend the dignified childhood of the children. The penalty should be further up, since such an abominable act may impair a child's childhood, therefore affecting a child's physical and emotional health. There are various disadvantages to this conduct in connection with child sexual abuse. The violation and murder in the kathua gang rape case did not influence the country's status since the crime rate has risen after that occurrence. It is not applied in practice what we read in the Act.

Cognitive Aspect

Child sexual abuse may cause internal incisions and bleeding based on the age and size of the child and the level of strength exerted. Danger to internal organs may develop in extreme circumstances, which may cause death, in certain cases. Child maltreatment may induce sexually transmitted illnesses and disorders. Due to a lack of vaginal fluid, the probability of infection is increased depending on the age of the kid. Also reported were vaginitis. Treatment: The first strategy to treating a victim of sexual abuse depends on several crucial factors: age at the time of presentation, treatment circumstances and co-morbid illnesses. The aim of therapy is to address existing problems in the field of mental health and avoid future problems.

Emotional Aspect

Child sexual abuse, including later-life psychopathology, may cause both short-term and long-term damage. Repeated or recurrent victims throughout adolescence and adulthood are a well known, long term deleterious impact. There have been causal links between childhood sexual abuse and numerous psychopathologies of adults, including criminality and suicide and drug misuse.

The criminal justice system is more common for guys who have been abused sexually as youngsters than for men with severe mental health conditions. It was discovered that intergenerational impacts had more issues, peer problems, and emotional problems than their parents among children who were victims of child sexual abuse. The societal stigma of child sexual abuse may make children more affected by psychological trauma than the harmful effects of child abuse, with supporting families, are less probable. Depression, somatization, anxiety, eating disorders, low self-esteem and sleep difficulties are indicators and consequences, including after-traumatic stress disorders. The results of this analysis will be obtained. Victims may leave school and social activities and have numerous learning and behaviour difficulties, including animal cruelty, ADHD, a disorder of conduct, oppositional defiant disorder (ODD), etc. Victims are allowed to withdraw from school and social activities. In adolescence, teenage pregnancy and unsafe sexual behaviour. Victims of child sexual abuse report roughly four times more damage to themselves. Post-traumatic Stress Disorder (PTSD) dissociation and disorder: The development of high levels of dissociative symptoms, including amnesia for memories of abuse, was shown in connection with abuse by children, including sex, particularly chronic abuse commencing at an early age. Having happened severe sexual abuse (penetration, many offenders, more than one year) was even more prevalent than that. In addition to dissociative identity (DID) and post-Traumatic Stress Disorder (PTSD), borderline personality disorder and eating disorganizations, including bulimia nervousa, may occur to survivors of child sexual abuse.

Social Aspect

The most striking stigmatic component is regrettable. Victims are facing dishonour and humiliation in society rather than offenders. They are accused of being abused. The stigmatization of the abused victims is quite severe and distressing. In the future life of the victim, stigmatization takes place more often in a non-abusive relationship. Significant per cent of abused children's parents do not counsel their children for societal stigma for health problems.

Conclusion

There has been wide-ranging discussion on the impacts of violent events like as sexual abuse as the implications of traumatic experiences in infancy are significantly connected with alterations in cognitive, emotional and behavioural malfunctions that may continue up to maturity. The ongoing pandemic of sexual abuse (SA) is culturally and societally-independent. Sexual abuse Brazil still needs further study on how the emotional and cognitive elements of SA victims are evaluated, since applications for assessments in the court setting are also increasing.

In general, compared with the near lack of judicial training, psychologists are better acquainted with clinical studies. The conduct of the forensic psychological assessment thus demands a thorough understanding and a profound knowledge of the grounds, purpose and application of psychological tools, as well as knowledge of the normal and abnormal psychological functioning of the person and a concept of law. It also needs consistent fields of psychology, developmental psychology, personality (traits and disorders), cognitive psychology (care, memory, thinking, etc., psychological processes), assessment procedures and forensic interview protocols with abused children.

The knowledge of these areas will help a psychologist to recognise how someone thinks (which is related with cognitive processes), how they feel and how they adjust the pattern of interaction with the environment, dependent on their emotional organisation and psychological characteristics. The ability to systematise the assessment of these populations by establishing a referential protocol will therefore provide more evidence on clinical, social and cognitive issues, support referencing more effectively, support in judiciary matters and preventive work in schools, and in the field of SA victims' mental health.

Author's Bio

Vidhi Krishali is an IV-year law student from Symbiosis Law School, Hyderabad. She has a keen interest in writing on contemporary social issues related to women and children. She has been a dedicated researcher and has published articles and journals in renowned Indian Law Journals and Blogs. She has also represented her university in many competitions in India as well as Internationally. She has done moots, debates as well as mediation competitions to instill a sense of learning. Keeping grades aside, she has been a firm supporter of bridging the gap between academics and the corporate sector. She is the Advisory Board Member and Ex- President of the Centre for Finance, Accountability, Corporate Governance and Transparency, SLS- Hyderabad, Vice-President of the Website and Public Relation and Media Center and Senior Member of the Student Council of SLS-Hyderabad.

CHAPTER THREE

DUE DILIGENCE TO MODERN HUMANITARIAN LAW

Author: Arnav Laroia, I Year of B.A.,LL.B(Hons.) From National Law University, Jodhpur.

<u>**ABSTRACT**</u>

International humanitarian law is a set of principles and guidelines aimed at reducing the negative consequences of armed conflicts. It protects individuals who aren't or aren't participating in conflicts, and it restricts fighting weaponry and methods. International humanitarian law is a subset of international law that controls international interactions. International law is included in treaties or conventions between nations, as well as customary norms, which are state practices regarded legally binding by them, and general principles. Despite the high esteem it maintains on a worldwide level, parties to certain conflicts continue to disregard IHL's principles on a scale that is reason for severe concern across the globe. Serious examination and thoughts on this sad element are required, and it is essential to determine the causes for these undesired activities. Despite the multiple challenges it faces, IHL has a unique and vital role to play in lessening the devastation of armed conflict for people and communities. States' commitment to respect and implement the Conventions is the most important first step in alleviating the suffering and needs of people affected by ongoing armed conflicts.

<u>**INTRODUCTION**</u>

International humanitarian law is a set of principles and guidelines aimed at reducing the negative consequences of armed conflicts. It protects individuals who aren't or aren't participating in conflicts, and it restricts fighting weaponry and methods. International humanitarian law is a subset of international law that controls international interactions. International law is included in treaties or conventions between nations, as well as customary norms, which are state practices regarded legally binding by them, and general principles. Internal tensions or disturbances, such as individual acts of violence, are not covered by IHL, which only applies to armed confrontations. Once a dispute has begun, the law applies to all parties equally, regardless of who began it. International humanitarian law differentiates between international and non-international armed confrontations. Seven decades after their inception, the 1949 Geneva Conventions have obtained worldwide ratification, frequent reaffirmation, and substantial absorption into domestic law and military doctrine. Armed forces apply International Humanitarian Law (IHL) on a regular basis to reduce the human cost of war. For many individuals, following the rules is a question of professional identity and personal principles. Despite significant improvement, however, noncompliance with IHL remains a challenging issue to tackle. Each transgression has major consequences for those involved, and when rule-breaking is common in a conflict, it has disastrous consequences not just for individuals but also for communities, cities, and regions. Despite the high esteem it maintains on a worldwide level, parties to certain conflicts continue to disregard IHL's principles on a scale that is reason for severe concern across the globe. Serious examination and thoughts on this sad element are required, and it is essential to determine the causes for these undesired activities. Despite the multiple challenges it faces, IHL has a unique and vital role to play in lessening the devastation of armed conflict for people and communities. States' commitment to respect and implement the Conventions is the most important first step in alleviating the suffering and needs of people affected by ongoing armed conflicts.

<u>MODERN CONFLICTS AND THEIR CONSEQUENCES</u>

For the better part of the previous decade, many regionalized conflicts have maintained their downward spiral of violence, often fueled by severe IHL breaches. Yemen is besieged by diseases, other significant health crises, starvation, and deteriorating infrastructure, and has become the world's most catastrophic humanitarian calamity. As a consequence of Syria's turbulence, displaced survivors of horrific violence are still living in deplorable conditions and are separated from their relatives. The most chronic disputes continue to drag life down and prevent healing, with some exhibiting symptoms of escalation. The scenario of Afghanistan, where civilian fatalities have increased despite heightened peace discussions, is a good example. The Tigray issue is another example of this, which has posed significant challenges for the Ethiopian government and other major African nations participating in the regional war. In many instances, such confrontations have resulted in extensive migration, leaving family members ignorant of one another's whereabouts or well-being. Many of those who have been transferred look to be in an eternal state of misery. The failure of the international system to maintain peace and security has shifted the emphasis of international engagement away from conflict resolution and toward humanitarian endeavors, among other things. As a consequence, a great deal of work has gone into negotiating humanitarian access, humanitarian pauses, local ceasefires, and civilian evacuations, among other things. While obtaining an agreement on humanitarian access and assistance to those in need is a positive thing, the political squabbles that often precede such meetings risk destroying the notion of impartial humanitarian intervention and running counter to its goal and purpose. As a consequence of these wars, the global humanitarian sector is on the point of imploding. Independent humanitarian organizations are challenged with tremendous humanitarian needs in an unprecedented number of concurrent crises throughout the globe. The gap between such needs and humanitarian actors' capacity to provide them is difficult to narrow.

DIFFICULTIES FOR INTERNATIONAL HUMANITARIAN LAW

Apart from the challenges that International Humanitarian Law confronts in today's world, there are a number of other factors that are exacerbating and prolonging the suffering caused by contemporary armed conflicts. People living in conflict-affected areas are more exposed to drought and other natural disasters as a result of climate change. The use of social media to vilify and instigate violence against communities is becoming increasingly common. Additionally, failing to accommodate for said disparities as far as how individuals of different age groups and genders experience abuse enables their specific needs to go unnoticed and unfulfilled. Accepting the applicability of International Humanitarian Law to all individuals affected by armed conflict, whatever of their actions, is critical for maintaining legal respect, even though it is a recurring difficulty in today's society. Another source of worry is and it is becoming increasingly difficult to engage conflicting parties in a debate about their obligations within international human rights law. When armed organizations split up and reform with new, sometimes ill-defined formations, and governments retreat from direct engagement in extraterritorial wars in favor of supporting other parties, apportioning blame for violations becomes more difficult. In order to promote conformity with the Act, it is also necessary to resolve the less evident obstacles in understanding and enforcing IHL. Furthermore, by loosening the interpretation of core principles of IHL to preserve the legitimacy of such an expedient action to take, States risk setting negative legal precedents and allowing subsequent entities to inflict agony beyond what has been militarily required or bearable to humanity. IHL's current problems extend well beyond rule infractions. Changes in war techniques, means, and locations continue to put treaty and customary law's adaptability to the test. As the globe becomes more urbanized, counterinsurgency and its effects on normal society, economy, and utilities have become a major concern. Furthermore, advancements in military hardware have both good and bad repercussions of global armed conflict law. Whatever the outcome of these occurrences, arguments, and conversations, critical assessments and perspectives are required: Weapon innovation may provide for unprecedented targeting precision plus options to complete annihilation; nonetheless, IHL requires considerable legal research and human decision-making.

<u>SUGGESTIONS AND CONCLUSION</u>

IHL provides a clear but strong message: all battles, even those between furious foes, have limits. It might be argued that current IHL laws, when supplemented with other international law principles, are adequate to ensure a minimal level of humanity in armed conflict. As a global community, we must protect the fundamentals while investigating new and unsolved issues. Any interpretation or development of the legislation should be based on the IHL provisions currently in place. It should never be used as a means of defamation. Perhaps most importantly, IHL norms can only avoid atrocities if all States take efforts to fulfil their legal obligations, if all participants to armed conflicts are committed to maintaining them, and if all actors with influence over those engaged in combat utilize it to guarantee that IHL is followed.

States have spent a lot of time and effort over the years, with the aid of other stakeholders, developing and implementing preventive measures in peacetime to guarantee improved respect for IHL. IHL has gradually being assimilated into military doctrine, both in academia and within the armed services. Domestic laws and regulations have progressively been approved or altered, and the necessary procedures to give effect to the IHL treaties' provisions have been put in place. Despite these advancements in prevention, a disregard for international humanitarian law during armed conflict continues to be a problem. Due to a lack of political will and practical skill, participants to an armed conflict, including States and armed groups, fail to comply with their legal obligations. While efforts to enhance IHL violation prevention and repression are important and should be continued, the subject of how to secure improved IHL compliance during armed conflicts requires and merits greater attention.

CHAPTER FOUR

THERAPY IN INDIA, WHILE STILL A TABOO, SHOULD BE A FUNDAMENTAL RIGHT

Author: Vranda Rellan, II Year of B.B.A.,LL.B from Symbiosis Law School Hyderabad.

Brief- Despite various preventive measures being taken, therapy is still a taboo in India and society still judge people for something that isn't their fault. There is still a long way to go in order to solve the mental health issue.

The issues of mental health, social isolation, and anxiety have never been more prominent than in the age of COVID-19. Because mental illnesses can have serious consequences if left untreated, it is critical to recognise and treat them. Suicides caused by depression are the second-most common cause of death in people aged 15 to 29 years old, according to a report published by the World Health Organization (WHO). This invalidates the stereotype that the illness only affects the elderly. According to the report, anyone, young or old, can suffer from depression or other mental illnesses. However, most people are hesitant to openly discuss mental illness, or even to acknowledge the possibility that they are suffering from it.

Why is mental health care such a complicated issue? The word covers a wide range of conditions, from ordinary transitory and acute anxiety and sadness to severe chronic disorders like schizophrenia or bipolar disease. Putting everything or everyone into one category is inaccurate and unfair.

CAUSES

The mental health of a person can vary throughout time, based on a variety of conditions. When a person's resources and coping abilities are stretched beyond their limits, their mental health may suffer. A variety of things can contribute to mental illness. The death of a loved one or the loss of one's job are both tragic events. Long-term stress, loneliness, poverty fear, and losing one's source of money are some of the more typical causes of serious mental illnesses in people.

MENTAL ILLNESS: STILL A TABOO IN INDIA

According to the WHO, 7.5 percent of Indians suffer from some form of mental illness, and it is predicted that by the end of this year, about 20% of India will be affected by mental illnesses. It is estimated that over 56 million Indians suffer from depression, with another 38 million suffering from anxiety disorders. India, on the other hand, appears to be lagging behind in terms of recognising and managing mental health and related issues.

Depression and anxiety crises are usually dismissed as small annoyances experienced primarily by the ultra-wealthy. Worse, people with mental illnesses tend to hide their problems for fear of being condemned and looked down upon by a conservative society. In India, shedding these negative characteristics and bringing about a culture shift could take several years.

Despite the progress made on the paper, there is still a pitiful lack of social infrastructure in place to deal with the problem, which decreases demand for care. Discrimination and social stigma are still present. They remain the most significant impediments to the use of mental health services.

OVERCOMING THE TABOO

Delaying or refusing care to those who need it the most could be the cause of innumerable fatalities throughout the age and geographical spectrum. To avoid a chain reaction of terrible events, the government might make mental health care more inexpensive and accessible to people of all income levels. In this regard, the Healthcare Act of 2017 is a positive step forward.

Workplace safety training should also cover how to treat co-workers, whether or not they have mental problems. Mental health training and monitoring can be a good supplement to behaviour-based safety programmes. People all around the country must show empathy for their fellow countrymen and women. While it may be unrealistic to expect a huge shift in people's conceptions of mental health and wellbeing, even minor improvements in behaviour and attitude will go a long way toward improving many people's mental health and well-being.

RIGHT TO HEALTH AS AN EXCLUSIVE FUNDAMENTAL RIGHT

Currently, the Indian Constitution does not specifically acknowledge the "right to health" as a basic right, despite Article 21 guaranteeing the protection of life and personal liberty. The Constitution (One Hundred and Twenty-Seventh Amendment) Bill, 2021, proposes to put new Article 21(B) into the Constitution. In accordance with international treaties, there has been an increasing call to recognise the "right to health" as a fundamental right. Several MPs have also advocated constitutional amendments in the past to support a rights-based approach to health.

The Bill was introduced in the Rajya Sabha in 2017. According to the Bill, the state is required to offer health protection to all residents, including disease prevention, treatment, and control, as well as access to needed medicines. According to the Bill, all residents should have access to basic health services, emergency medical treatment, and mental healthcare.

CONCLUSION

This particular age-old societal principle is applicable to everyone in India. It transcends gender, caste, religion, socioeconomic status, and geographic boundaries. It rules supreme in managing people's choices because if people's weaknesses become publicly known, they would be subjected to judgement, gossip, and drama. It also prevents much-needed mental health care from being provided.

There is an urgent need for a justiciable mechanism to protect all Indian citizens' health, including illness prevention, treatment, and control, as well as access to free or low-cost medical care, diagnostics, and vital drugs. Making the Right to Health a basic right will help us get closer to that goal. The state has a responsibility to provide free or low-cost healthcare to all of its residents.

The future of mental health concerns in India may not be decided by the sufferers, but by the society that surrounds them. However, if mental health care taboos persist, it will reflect poorly on society rather than the individual.

CHAPTER FIVE

LEGALIZATION OF PROSTITUTION

Author: Ravina Raj, I year of B.A.,LL.B. from NMIMS, Hyderabad.

Slavery still exists, but now it only applies to women and its name is prostitution. The source of the English word "prostitution" is the Latin verb "prostituere," which meaning "to expose openly." Prostitution is defined as the sale of one's sexual services for a fee. When it comes to violence against women, men are more likely to target women than women, which makes prostitution a gender-specific issue. It would be naive, however, to assert that men are immune to sexual exploitation and violence. When we talk about the issues with India's prostitution business, we often overlook the plight of transgender persons. By exploiting the socially and economically poor, prostitution produces billions of dollars around the world.

Background

In India, prostitution has been conducted for millennia. In reality, sex workers are attributed to as apsaras in various Hindu mythical passages. The devdasi system existed throughout the pre-colonial period, and it was widespread practise with hindus who start donating their female kid as only a mark of their devotion to god. Devdasi literally means "devoted to the divine," meaning that they were betrothed to God and were not required to marry mortals.

They were sexually liberated ladies who succeeded in a range of creative areas, including dance and music. Colonialism, on the other hand, brought with it a system of exploitation and tyranny. The British began to reflect their own cultural restraints on these women, changing the basics of sexual freedom, womanhood, artistry, and culture into devotion, bhakti, and etc, and all these women began to be abused by temple priests when aristocracy faded and colonialism ended. As a consequence, they are at risk of sexual exploitation and poverty. In India, this is one of the earliest types of prostitution.

Prostitution's Causes

A lot has changed for women who worked in palaces, harems, and brothels since the Delhi sultanate empire collapsed. Poverty is a major contributor to prostitution. Being economically independent as a woman in patriarchal India is challenging, especially if she has been denied an education, freedom, and the opportunity to use her gifts. So, prostitution is the only source of cash for them.

In India, women are more vulnerable to sexual abuse because of the traditional society's view of them as nothing more than an object or a resource to be used. As a result of the caste system in India, many women are forced into prostitution and left to rot in degraded society. Additionally, prostitution might be caused by a lack of sex education or kidnapped.

The practice of sex trade

In order to make a case for legalising prostitution, one must first acknowledge its existence and necessity in society. This is especially true in India, where talking about sex is still a major taboo. Prostitution is regularly attacked as morally repugnant and should be outlawed by a variety of groups and individuals. Even though most people think prostitution is wrong, the sex industry, like all others, depends on demand. We just don't see it. If demand increases, the business succeeds in commercialising its products.

Red light districts, private massage parlours, and the internet have all become places where people can buy sex for a fee. As a result of criminalising the practise, the real victims of sexual exploitation would be denied justice, opening the door for more oppression and violence against the industry.

Indian laws related to prostitution

To be sure, prostitution as a whole is not prohibited by India's penal code, but some behaviours that constitute a large component of prostitution are.

i. Prostitution soliciting in public places.

ii. Hotel prostitution is a sort of prostitution.

iii. Thirdly, owning a brothel and running it.

iv. Pimping.

v. Hire a sex worker to help you prostitution.

vi. Arranging a sexual encounter with a client

According to the 1956 Immoral Traffic (Prevention) Act, a prostitute is someone who profited from the sexual abuse or exploitation of a female for financial gain. A bill known as SITA was signed into law by the U.S. Congress in 1956. According to this guideline prostitutes are authorised to begin their careers in secret but are not allowed to do their business in public. A sex encounter in public may result in a client's arrest, according to the legislation.

Within 200 yards of a public place, a woman cannot engage in commercial sex. It is illegal for sex workers in India to be regulated by the country's existing labour laws, but they are entitled to the same rights as any other Indian citizen.

The original law was amended in 1986 by the Immoral Traffic (Prevention) Statute. If prostitutes are spotted advertising or luring others, they will be penalised under this law. In addition, call girls are not allowed to reveal their personal information to the public. If they are detected, they might be sentenced to six months in prison and fined.

Sex workers who engage in sexual activity with clients within 200 yards of a public place can be jailed for up to three months and fined up to $1,000. Those found in sexual conduct with a minor face a prison sentence of up to ten years in prison. Also at fault are pimps and those who make a living off the work of prostitutes. An adult man may be found guilty of prostitution if he lives with a prostitute.

In the event that he fails to prove his innocence, he will be sentenced to between two and four years in prison. According to the preamble of SITA (1956), which was later changed to ITPA (1986), the purpose of the legislation was to pay attention to the Trafficking Convention. in accordance with an international treaty signed in New York on the 9th of May 1950, Parliament adopted this legislation as An Act to legislate to prohibit the sale of immoral goods and services to women and girls.

Constitutional questions were raised about ITPA in the landmark case, "The State of Uttar Pradesh versus Kaushaliya." This case was a test case for the ITPA. A few of the prostitutes were asked to quit their positions in Kanpur in order to maintain the city's decorum, according to the evidence.

India's High Court of Allahabad found that Section 20 of the Act violates Article 14 of the Indian Constitution as well as Article 19(1) subclauses (d) and (e). A legal distinction could be drawn between a prostitute and a disruptive individual, hence the Act was judged to be valid.

The objective of the Act, which is to promote social order and decency, is also consistent with the Act. It is the goal of the act to preserve the public's morality and decorum, as well as to rescue fallen women and girls and provide them with the opportunity to reintegrate into society. As a result of the law, the central government is empowered to establish a special court for the adjudication of cases involving prostitution.

Criticism of this act

Many SITA policies discriminated against trafficking victims and penalised victims rather than perpetrators, contrary to the trafficking treaties. Trafficking conventions do not allow for any penalties to be imposed on prostitution victims. According to Article 1, anybody who: (1) obtains, entices, or leads away another individual for the purpose of prostitution, even with that individual's consent; or (2) exploits a person's prostitution to satisfy the needs of another, even with that individual's consent, is subject to penalties.

Under Article 2 of the Convention, the Parties to the Convention further

Adopt a policy of criminalising anyone who: runs or controls a brothel; knowingly funds or participates in the funding of a brothel; purposefully lets or leases a building or another site, or any portion of it, for the prostitution of other people's bodies.

A prostitute victim cannot be considered a criminal in any of these statutes, which are established in the convention. True criminals who are involved in recruiting, enticing or trafficking someone for prostitution were the target of the legislation. The goal of the original international convention was to stop the trafficking of people into prostitution by outlawing and discouraging all types of sexual exploitation.

Prostitution and commercial sex work can still be done without the permission or freedom of the individual. As far as prostitution is concerned, the ITPA in India neither prohibits nor criminalises its practise in its totality. However, despite this, there are numerous policies that discriminate against sex workers, and even punish them. SITA's most important features are outlined in the following sentences: Section 2(f) defines prostitution as the act of a female providing her body for sexual intercourse with a client in exchange for monetary gain.

This definition does not include men or transgender people. The maximum term for a woman who engages in prostitution within 200 yards of an open area is now three months in prison. Women can be imprisoned for up to a year for the same crime, but pimps can only be imprisoned up to three months. This is a discriminatory sentence clause in the statute. The law's primary flaw is that it focuses solely on street prostitution, neglecting to address other forms of prostitution. On top of that, the "middlemen" in the industry get off easy. There are no legal protections for sex workers in closed-door prostitution, which is implied to be legal in the statute.

Fundamentally, this restriction violates society's decorum since it views prostitution as wicked and repulsive. With that said, it is nevertheless true that engaging in sexual activity when it is done in accordance with applicable laws and precautions is not harmful.

Due to the widespread taboo around sexual activity in our society, it is considered sinful and deplorable to engage in prostitution or hire a sex worker.

The Indian culture is unable to accept the reality of sexual assault occurring as a result of existing sex norms in the community and those who believe and continue to live on these standards of behaviour. There's little doubt that the law's inability to face the underlying issue is demonstrated by its inability to punish those who engage in sexually motivated behaviour, which leads to prostitution.

A Proposed Amendment in 2006

The Immoral Traffic (Prevention) Act was reformed in 2006. The elements that make prospecting clients a criminal have been removed from the modified draught. In this approach, the penalties will be tougher and the fines greater. As a result of this proposal, a person who goes to a brothel for the intention of sexually exploiting a victim of human trafficking will face at least three months in prison or a fine in the amount of Rs. 20,000.

In order to combat human trafficking, the bill establishes federal and state authority. Anyone found guilty of human trafficking for the purpose of prostitution will be punished under the term "person trafficking."

Article 21 of the Constitution of India Personal freedom and safety are highlighted in this article. If a person is deprived of his or her life or liberty, it must be done in line with the law.

The case was Budhadev Karmaskar v. West Bengal. Sex workers are people who need to be treated with respect and dignity, according to the court ruling in this instance. No one has the right to physically harm them in any way. Also, the verdict exposed the hardships and misery endured by sex workers. The Court believes that these women are not forced to prostitute themselves out of choice or pleasure, but rather because of economic and societal pressure.

Federal and state governments were instructed by the court to enrol sex workers in vocational and technical courses and to create rehabilitation centres in order to improve their job prospects. Immoral Traffic Prevention Act Section 21 requires the State Government to establish and operate protective homes, which are regulated and licenced by them. Protective housing should be investigated by a competent authority. Only a limited number of these permits were available and they could not be transferred. According to Section 23, the state has the ability to enact auxiliary legislation on matters such as the licencing, management, and maintenance of these residences.

Code of Criminal Procedure (CPC) of India

An important part of IPC's anti-trafficking provisions deals with the trafficking of women and girls into prostitution under duress, which is expressly forbidden. Prostitution or illicit intercourse with a minor is a crime punishable by up to ten years in prison under the IPC if it is committed by anyone who buys, sells, or acquires the possession of a minor, or who knows that such a minor is likely to be employed or used for such purposes at any time in the future.

A person who brings a young woman under the age of twenty-one into India with the intent or knowledge that she will be forced or seduced to engage in sexual relations with another individual is subject to up to ten years in prison and a fine under the Indian Penal Code, which defines cross-border prostitution trafficking.

For the IPC's rape provision, a brothel prisoner is likewise covered. According to the International Penal Code, rape is defined as an act of sexual intercourse with a woman who does not want it, or with her consent but under threat or fear that she would be harmed, or with her consent if she is under the age of 16.

The minimum term for rape is seven years in prison, according to the IPC. There are new regulations in place for brothel owners and staff members, as well as for those customers who have sex with children or women who are being held in brothels.

<u>The following are the types of crime associated with prostitution and human trafficking</u>

    i. Procuration of Minor girls (section 366-A IPC).

    ii. Importation of Girls (Section-366-B IPC).

    iii. Selling of Girls for prostitution (Section-372 IPC).

    iv. Buying of Girls for Prostitution (Section-373 IPC).

    v. Immoral Trafficking (Prevention) Act 1956.

    vi. Child Marriage Retrain Act, 1929.

The fundamental issue with these rules is that the public perceives prostitution as immoral and disgusting, as well as a threat to society's decorum. However, the reality remains that indulging in sex work with safeguards and laws does not do any harm to anybody. Furthermore, prostitution is viewed as immoral, and sex workers are regarded as disgusting, merely because sex is a big taboo in our culture, and the producers and consumers of sex in a regulated manner is something to be despised.

The Indian culture is unable to comprehend the reality of sexual assault occurring as a result of existing sex norms in the society and individuals believing and continuing to survive on these standards. The fact that the act attempts to penalise behaviours that lead to prostitution reflects the law's uneasiness in confronting the true issue and makes transitory and half-hearted modifications in tackling the issue.

Another significant feature of Indian prostitution laws that goes unnoticed is that these laws fail to recognise that it is not just women who are victims of sexual abuse, but also males and transgender persons who are victims of sexual violence, exploitation, and oppression

Legalisation of prostitution

Prostitute legalisation has been hotly debated in India. Controlling prostitution is necessary because the chances of its elimination are small. It is allowed in Canada, the United States and other countries including France and Germany, as well as in Denmark and Wales to engage in prostitution.

Bodineries are allowed to use HR agencies to market and make job offers in Germany because the industry is not only taxed but also regulated. As of 2016, all prostitution in Germany required a permit and a certificate of registration for prostitutes, as part of new legislation designed to protect these women.

When the profession is regulated and the needs of sex workers are taken into account, the harm to these workers is reduced, and the system as a whole is better protected against abuse and exploitation. In addition to the dangers of HIV AIDS and other sexually transmitted diseases, these workers often suffer police aggression, a decrease in pay, harassment, and other difficulties. Prostitution was proposed to be legalised by the Supreme Court in 2009.

Providing legal status to prostitutes has sparked much debate in India. Controlling prostitution is necessary because the chances of its elimination are small. Prostitution is regulated and legal in Canada, France, Germany, Denmark, and Wales.

It's legal and taxed in Germany, for example, and brothels are allowed to advertise and make job offers through human resources departments. In 2016, Germany also implemented new legislation to protect prostitutes, requiring a permit for all prostitution trades and a certificate of registration for prostitutes.

As a result of this form of system, which is more heavily regulated and takes into account the protections of sex workers, less harm is inflicted on sex workers, and better law enforcement protects the system from abuse and exploitative. In addition to the dangers of HIV AIDS and other sexually transmitted diseases, these workers suffer police assault, a loss in pay, harassment, and other difficulties. Prostitution was proposed to be legalised by the Supreme Court in 2009.

The following are some of the reasons why prostitution should be legalised

i. Legalizing prostitution protects children from being sexually victimised. The number of child prostitutes in the world is at around 10 million. Nearly every country has some form of child prostitution, although Asia and South America have the worst problems. Minors can be kept out of the system by enforcing rigorous industry regulations.

ii. There would be a significant reduction in the incidence of HIV/AIDS among sex workers with mandatory health screenings. Unplanned pregnancies can be avoided, as can other health hazards, with the use of effective birth control methods. In order to keep the workplace as clean and sanitary as possible, it is important to conduct regular health checks and impose strict restrictions. Both the sex industry and the general public would gain from making condoms readily available.

iii. Legalizing prostitution will bring the system up to date and enhance it. When middlemen and pimps are eliminated, sex workers can earn more while the unlawful and exploitative components are minimised.

iv. It will reduce sexual violence, rapes, and other forms of sexual assault because people will look for a legal and easier means to satisfy their sexual needs. In Queensland, for example, rape rates rose by 149% when brothels were shut down.

v. Forced prostitution must be abolished completely.

vi. The prostitute industry in India is estimated to be worth $8.4 billion dollars. The government will be compelled to legalise and tax the procedure as a form of incentive.

vii. Employee rights shall be protected. Workers in the sexual prostitution industry should have the same rights as everybody else, regardless of whether or not standard labour rules apply to them.

viii. Legalizing prostitution protects children from being sexually victimised. The number of child prostitutes in the world is at around 10 million. Nearly every country has some form of child prostitution, although Asia and South America have the worst problems. Minors can be kept out of the system by enforcing rigorous industry regulations.

ix. There would be a significant reduction in the incidence of HIV/AIDS among sex workers with mandatory health screenings. Unplanned pregnancies can be avoided, as can other health hazards, with the use of effective birth control methods. In order to keep the workplace as clean and sanitary as possible, it is important to conduct regular health checks and impose strict restrictions. Both the sex industry and the general public would gain from making condoms readily available.

x. Legalizing prostitution will bring the system up to date and enhance it. When middlemen and pimps are eliminated, sex workers can earn more while the unlawful and exploitative components are minimised.

xi. It will reduce sexual violence, rapes, and other forms of sexual assault because people will look for a legal and easier means to satisfy their sexual needs. In Queensland, for example, rape rates rose by 149% when brothels were shut down.

xii. Forced prostitution must be abolished completely.

xiii. The prostitute industry in India is estimated to be worth $8.4 billion dollars. The government will be compelled to legalise and tax the procedure as a form of incentive.

xiv. Employee rights shall be protected. Sex workers, even though they don't fall within the jurisdiction of traditional labour laws, deserve the same rights as any other citizen or worker.

<u>Conclusion</u>

In a culture where prostitution has been a long-standing profession and is still prospering as a business, it would be unwise to turn a blind eye to it and pretend the system and its problems do not exist. Decriminalizing sex work and making it legal will give a better life for sex workers by providing higher earnings, health security, and protection. Not only that, but as a society, it will be a progressive move that will remove many societal ills such as child prostitution, rape, and so on. Sex trade is a widely visible reality in our nation, and by identifying it as a legal business with certain standards and protections, all parties involved may gain. A more complete legislative framework, as well as the acceptance of all protective procedures, will only serve to benefit society.

<u>Author's Bio</u>

Hello!! My name is Ravina Raj, a law student from NMIMS, Hyderabad. I was born and brought up in Ranchi, Jharkhand. I'm always interested in writing about women's rights and issues.

My friends describe me as a easy going girl, a good listener, problem solver and many more. There's so much to learn more in this world.

CHAPTER SIX

FREEBIES CULTURE IN INDIAN POLITICS

Author: Nipun, B.B.A.,LL.B from Geeta Institute of law

INTRODUCTION

Freebies are items that are provided without charge or cost. In Indian politics, it has been rampant. During election season, it is a well-known and prevalent habit . Freebie politics has been an important aspect of electoral campaigns in recent years, and the situation is no different in the upcoming assembly elections in five states: Uttar Pradesh, Uttarakhand, Goa, Punjab, and Manipur.

Freebies are one of the most profitable ways for political parties to entice voters. Freebies were offered by both the Congress and the BJP in the 2019 general election. There has been a shift in the way freebies are distributed. Free water, free power, and free health care are no longer attractive.

MAIN BODY

The word "freebie" is not new in politics, although it has become fashionable in recent years. During the previous 20 years, India has undergone various developments in several fields. Hinduism and Islam are the two main cornerstones of Indian politics. Politicians do not gain votes from voters based on work done or challenges facing the country such as employment, inflation, poverty, or government work done during their time period.

Now, let's talk about the culture of freebies. First and foremost, the question arises in the minds of ordinary people: what does it mean? Freebie culture is simply defined as giving something to individuals who are in desperate need without charging them any money. Our political parties, on the other hand, are doing it solely to obtain votes from voters. It is solely done to entice voters to vote for them. Such pledges are prevalent throughout political campaigns.

Yes, it is undoubtedly beneficial if the government provides free education or health care to all citizens. It will strengthen the fundamental framework of our society, yet political parties prefer to give people free tablets, cellphones, and scotties instead.

During the election campaign in Punjab, the Aam Aadmi Party promised to distribute 300 free units of energy to everyone. This results in the party's victory, or other factors may be at play. In Delhi, the ruling party follows a similar policy. However, the Haryana government is offering free iPads to students for educational purposes. If used properly, this is a beneficial thing. All ladies who have completed their 12th grade will receive a free scooty from the state government of Uttar Pradesh. The Bihar government is offering sewing machines to every women so that they can earn a living. The government has taken a positive move.

NEGATIVE EFFECTS OF FREEBIE'S

The impacts of the freebie culture on the country are discussed:

These types of activities have a negative impact on the country, our economy, and our inhabitants. Now go over each one in detail :-

1. Burden on economy: giving away free things unnecessarily can be a burden and have a negative impact on our economy. Demand and supply will be negatively affected.
2. Inefficient resource use: by providing free resources such as electricity, people may become complacent in their use. They will use needlessly even when it is not required. This will result in inefficient use of the resources available to us.
3. People will become lazy: If everything is provided for free, people will become lazy because they will not work and will believe that the government will provide them with everything. They will become completely reliant on the government for everything.
4. Leading the country to famine: Because the government gives people free things, their treasury will be depleted, potentially leading to famine. Sri Lanka is an example of a country that, despite its problems, does not distribute free goods to its citizens.
5. Reduces people's productivity: If a person receives free goods from the government, he or she will either not work or will work less.

ARGUMENTS IN FAVOUR OF FREEBIE

Now we'll look at some of the advantages of the freebies culture:

1. Facilitates growth: Some studies show that when a government provides things to people and spends money on them, the country grows. If a government spends money on health and education, for instance. In the near future, this will reveal the benefits.

2.Promotes Industry: States such as Tamil Nadu and Bihar are well-known for providing sewing machines, saris, and bicycles to women, but they do so with budget funds, boosting industry sales.

3. Important for meeting expectations: Some states in India, such as Bihar and Jharkhand, are underdeveloped, but the people there meet all of their expectations. As a result of their lack of education, they rely entirely on the government.

4. Assists countries with a lower level of development and a higher proportion of the population living in poverty, such freebies have become necessary to provide for the people's upliftment.

ARGUMENTS AGAINST FREEBIE

1. Freebies erode the fundamental foundation of macroeconomic stability, freebie politics influences expenditure priorities, and outlays remain centred on subsidies of some kind.

2. Impact on States' Fiscal Situation: Freebies have an impact on the public purse, as most Indian states are in dire financial straits with limited revenue resources.States' finances will deteriorate if money is spent on ostensibly political purposes.

3. Free and Fair Election: Before elections, promises of irrational freebies from public funds sway voters, disrupt the level playing field, and taint the election process.It's the equivalent as paying voters in terms of unethical behaviour.

4. Diverting Resources Away from Environmental and Sustainable Growth, Renewable Energy, and More Efficient Public Transportation Systems: When freebies involve giving away free power, or a set amount of free power, water, or other consumer products, resources are diverted away from environmental and sustainable growth, renewable energy, and more efficient public transportation systems.

CONCLUSION

It is beneficial to have a gratis culture if it is used properly. It must be used for individuals who are in desperate need of basic necessities. It must not be used by political parties in a way that lowers election competition between them. Elections must be held in a free and fair manner in order to benefit society and to assist the needy.

CHAPTER SEVEN

REDUCING ARMED FORCES SPECIAL POWERS ACT IS A BOON OR BANE?

Author: Lavanya KS, IV year of B.A.,LL.B. from Chennai Dr. Ambedkar Government Law College, Pudupakkam

ABSTRACT

The acts of parliament grant special powers to Indian armed forces, state police forces, and paramilitary forces. In those areas declared as disturbed areas in that place, the Armed Forces Special Powers Act provision can be extended which gives special power and immunity to all security forces. Powers enjoyed by the Indian army, state, and central police forces gave the power to shoot, kill, search houses, Destroy any property, and even arrest persons without a warrant. All these actions provide security forces with legal immunity and are given enormous powers by the act. While the Government of India and its security forces argued its needed legislation to tackle military or insurgency in India's Conflict Zones There was also criticism of the law. It alleged that security forces often misused these special powers to commit gross violence against human rights in conflict zones such as J&K, Northeast India, and the state of Punjab. According to these allegations, Indian security forces carried out fake encounters, rapes & Molestation, Torture & abduction. While covering up these human rights violations special powers and legal immunity were granted under AFSPA.

KEYWORDS:- AFSPA, draconian law, Nagaland, Naga Insurgency, reduce AFSPA in three regions.

INTRODUCTION

Those who Oppose AFSPA can even refer to a Draconian law (which has no place in Constitution Democracy). This controversial nature of AFSPA traces back to its Colonial Origin. This law was used by the British to counter the Quit India Movement & post Independence. India implemented the same law to tackle the Naga insurgency that broke out in the 1950s. Post-independence, AFSPA was introduced in 1958 to tackle the Naga insurgency in the northeast region. Later it extended to several northeast states such as Assam, Manipur, Mizoram, Tripura, and Meghalaya. In the 1980s the Khalistan movement broke out in Punjab so AFSPA also extended here as well. In 1987 Jammu and Kashmir insurgency broke out so AFSPA provision extended to J&J as well. But today AFSPA provision was removed in Punjab, Tripura, Meghalaya, and Mizoram because of declining insurgency it was revoked AFSPA. It continues to operate in the above states As sam, Jammu and Kashmir, Man, your, and Nagaland. Several strong observations were made against AFSPA by the supreme court, National Human Rights Commission, Second Administrative Reforms Committee as well as several committees such as the BP Jeevan Reddy committee, and Santosh Hegde Committee. Justice Verma Committee was constituted after Nirbaya Gang Rape Case. It had noted that the draconian law of AFSPA leads to a gross violation of Human rights. Conflict zones include fake encounters, custodial torture, rape, and molestation as a result law attracts a lot of controversies.

CEASE AFSPA IS A NECESSARY EVIL!

The government of India and security forces feels that law like AFSPA is needed in conflict zones as security forces operate in hostile conditions and they do seek legal immunity to allow them to function freely without fear of being targeted by false accusations. Now the killing of civilians by the army is regulated in this debate against AFSPA. To a strong call from civil society, human rights activists as well as local people from the northeast for the repeal of a controversial law which has given tremendous power to security forces.

In the Mon district of Nagaland para, special forces in the army which deployed in the region for counter-insurgency operation along with a unit of Assam rifles to target Naga insurgents have been deployed in the northeast, not just as a border guarding force with Myanmar. It was also deployed in counter-insurgency and was placed under the operational command of the Indian army. Two security forces jointly conduct joint security operations to target insurgents in the region and such one planned operation mistakenly killed several innocent civilians.

As per the report, the army received intelligence that a group of Naga insurgents moving into the Mon district while targeting them have mistakenly opened fire at a truck and six workers in a coal mine are killed. Following the killing of civilians, violence broke out in the region. People from nearby villages target cannons or rifles of the Indian army. During this violence, nine more civilians were killed by security forces and even soldiers lost their lives.

So killing 15 civilians by security forces led to an outburst of anger in Nagaland. The state government and the Indian army have already ordered their investigation into this failed security operation.

Even the union home minister angrily promises to investigate by setting up a high-level special investigation team. It led to a renewal of calls to repeal the AFSPA which gave enormous power to the Indian army and questioned the Naga insurgency. Even as a rifle counter-insurgency duties in the northeast. For several decades alleged special powers granted to security forces under AFSPA led to the gross human right violation. There is a strong demand to repeal AFSPA. This demand read the latest incident in Nagaland.

NAGA INSURGENCY

It traces back its origin pre-independence 1947, during British rule they found out warfighting skills in naga tribes. They recruited them during the first world war which was trained by the British and fought for them to gain political exposure after fighting in different parts of the world. So these naga soldiers formed the first naga political union known as the naga can club in 1918. This naga raised demand with British naga-inhabited areas (India and Burma) kept separate from India and sought independence in the Naga area. Members of the naga club raised this political demand to consider naga to have a different culture from India.

The Naga club met the Simon commission in 1928 and raised the demand for a separate nation for the Nagas. Later the second world war broke out again. The British used them to fight against them and nagas became more political. Some Naga leaders established Naga National Council, 1in 946. To take forward nationalist demands of nagas As India moves towards independence again Naga National Council asks for a separate nation for nagas.

To satisfy their demand, the British government worked out the Akbar Hydari agreement in June 1947. Through this, the British made concessions of political and constitutional autonomy for Naga inhabited areas set to be included in part of independent India. This agreement was accepted by dew only and many rejected this. Even before India became independent, the Naga national council declared unilateral independence from India, in 1947. After India gained independence and the Naga national council took violent insurgency against India to liberate Naga inhabited areas in India, Myanmar established greater Nagaland or Naga limb.

GOAL TO UNITE THEM

The goal of the Naga insurgency is to unite all Naga inhabited areas not just in Nagaland but also in Naga areas found in Assam, Manipur, Mizoram, and Myanmar the violent insurgency broke out in the northeast. To tackle the Naga insurgency India deployed security forces and enacted AFSPA, 1958 which gave special powers to the Indian army and security forces.

When the Naga insurgency broke out Nagaland was not a separate state it was still part of Assam. When AFSPA was introduced to tackle naga insurgency it essentially implemented other than stateAssamssam to cover naga insurgency affected regions.

Later AFSPA extended to other northeast states when another insurgency broke out. The first northeast insurgency was the Naga insurgency. As a result of security, operations carried out by the Indian Army under special powers of AFSPA India manage to weaken the Naga insurgency to an extent and try to use the opportunity to work out a peaceful solution through negotiation.

FULFILL POLITICAL ASPIRATION

To fulfill the political aspiration of naga India established Nagaland as a separate state and statehood were guaranteed in 1963. But this step by India failed to satisfy the Naga insurgency and continue for a few more years. By this time, the Naga insurgency was led by Naga National Council to establish a strong base in Myanmar and East Pakistan.

1971 East Pakistan fell and India helped in the liberation of Bangladesh. Naga insurgency lost key bases leading to weakening. India again tried to negotiate politically and India worked out the Shillong Accord 1975 with Naga national council. Through the Shillong accord, the government of India again made political concessions to give more autonomy to the Naga region. To bring the Naga insurgency to a peaceful resolution.

Just like the Akbar Hydari Agreement, the Shillong Accord is a failure. Few leaders accepted the accord and most went on to establish the national socialist council Nagaland in 1980. Its threat to India and managed to establish a haven in Myanmar and Bangladesh. Later in 1988, a group of the national socialist council of Nagaland split up due to ideological and different national socialist councils in Nagaland.

India achieved a breakthrough in 2009 when friendly relations with Bangladesh headed by the prime minister Sheik Hassina under the party Awami league very close to India cracked various northeast insurgents safe in Bangladesh.

NAGA PEACE PROGRESS

2015 framework agreement on Naga peace process signed between the government of India and National socialist council of Nagaland Isak Muivah faction to begin negotiation between Naga peace accord. However, the Khaplang faction is now against India by establishing a haven in Myanmar with the support of China.

Also, negotiate with naga groups to lead this negotiation. Government appoints former Intelligence Bureau officer R.N.Ravi special interlocutor of government and even appoint as governor of Nagaland. He had the experience to deal with naga insurgency and he was leading the peace process on behalf of the government of India.

Between 2015 and 2020 several rounds of talks took place between the governor of Nagaland and the leaders of the national socialist council of Nagaland Isak much and several other groups of Naga groups and political outfits.

PROBLEMS WITH GOVERNMENT

The last one and half years have deadened due to differences between R.N.Ravi and other naga groups. Peace talk failed and to go forward the government of India funds the national socialist council for Nagaland Isak much demand to be unacceptable. They demand a separate flag and a separate Constitution within the overall ambit of the constitution of India while the Indian government gives more autonomy and special status it is unwilling to accept this demand.

Ravi alleged that isak continued its violence and extortion. Naga outfits demand the government of India remove Ravi as an interlocutor. A few months ago he stepped down as interlocutor and was appointed as Governor of Tamil Nadu. Later the Central Government appointed retired IB officer A.K.Mishra as the new interlocutor. Despite these changes, peace talks did not make any changes due to unacceptable demands by naga outfits.

BIG ANNOUNCEMENT

The Union home affairs ministry has announced AFSPA law was reduced from three states to the northeast part of India. It gives powers to the army, state,e, and central police forces to tackle insurgency in disturbed areas. It has given the power to forces to search houses and destroy any property likely to be used by insurgents declared to be disturbed areas of insurgency by the union home affairs ministry. This law led to a lot of human rights violations and illegal killings in the past in multiple states. The recent one is in Nagaland Mon district that's why this law faces a lot of opposition in most states of the northeast part of India. This law gives security forces legal immunity from their actions in the disturbed areas which have led to all these protests.

As per notification given by the union home affairs ministry, they said AFSPA was removed from 15 police station areas in seven districts of Nagaland, 15 police station areas in 6 districts of Manipur, 23 districts entirely and one district partially in Assam. So in three states, AFSPA is being partially withdrawn in Nagaland, Assam, and Manipur.

The Union home minister Amit Shah said that the withdrawal of AFSPA is an indication that security situations are fast and improving in the northeast part of the country. Government peace efforts are bringing good results. It might come as a surprise for some people because nothing happened in the last few days. The most recent related to AFSPA is one in Nagaland Mon district in December 2021.

When in an army operation six civilians and residents attacked the army installation led to multiple losses of lives. After the Nagaland state assembly passed a resolution for repeal of AFSPA. Such resolutions are not binding on the union government. They decide on a disturbed area for AFSPA. Where AFSPA has been withdrawn in Nagaland and still imposed in Mon district, the district which killed civilians is still under AFSPA and part of disturbed areas.

CONCLUSION

In 2015, the government finally started to remove AFSPA in major parts of the northeast part of the region. They were removed in Tripura and Meghalaya and partially from Arunachal Pradesh.

Reducing conflicts in the northeast region. The central government has signed multiple agreements in the past few years in the northeast specifically to bring peace to the region.

- Bodo accord 2030

- Karbi Anglong 2021 in Assam
- National Liberation Front of Tripura agreement 2019 brings militants into the mainstream of Tripura.
- Bru-Reang refugee agreement 2020 to the resettlement of these refugees in the state of Tripura.

Recently, the chief minister of Assam and Meghalaya signed an agreement to resolve the outstanding disputes regarding boundaries between Assam and Meghalaya. Withdrawal of AFSPA in the northeast just seems to be a step in the same progression as the government of India has taken in the past few years. The first committee set up by the central government suggested repeal of AFSPA Jeevan Reddy Committee 2004 was set up by the UPA government but its recommendations were not accepted by the government.

Improved security situation:- 2021- 74% lesser incidence of militancy in the northeast compared to 2014. Even the death of our security personnel has fallen considerably. Fallen by 60% deaths of civilians 84%. All things considered, the union home affairs ministry thought this is a perfect time to repeal AFSPA and bring back normalcy to these parts of northeast India.

" THERE ARE FAR BETTER THINGS AHEAD THAN WE EVER BEHIND"

CHAPTER EIGHT

A TALE OF FORBIDDEN LOVE

Author: Shruti Tejwani from Amity University, Chhattisgarh.
Co-author: Vyakhya Gomasta from Amity University, Chhattisgarh.

"Marriage should be between a spouse and a spouse, not a gender and a gender."

-Hendrik Hertzberg

Three years ago, Section 377 was scrapped off the Indian Penal Code. Since then, things have drastically changed as our judiciary openly accepted the LGBTQ+ community. More people from the community have come out to their close ones. There have been open conversations about and with the community.

However, when we talk about social acceptance, privileges, and rights the community has, there isn't much of a change. Many people still view homosexuality as a disorder. As a result, same-sex couples are still fighting for their rights, legal legitimacy, and respect!

One of the reasons behind this discrimination is that our society is kin-based. Here, marriage is viewed as an arrangement to procreate, extend the family to bear heirs to the family property. In Indian society, family is considered the most important institution, which goes by "blood is thicker than water".

This traditional picture of marriage became a social and a religious norm governing marriage in our society. Thus, rejecting the idea of a union that wouldn't produce heirs to further the family's name. Hence, when two people of the same sex claim to be attracted towards each other and to be in love people treat them to be mentally ill.

It would be an unfair and crude violation of human rights, in today's era, to continue to accept this traditional thought of marriage. There are various instances of humiliation and hatred suffered by queer couples irrespective of place.

This picture depicts the miseries of queer couples which have now become a mere topic of political debates and campaigns.

Justice, equality, liberty, and fraternity form the pillars of our constitution. The Judiciary has upheld the Right to privacy as a fundamental right under Article 21 of the constitution. Considering the present scenario, however, these privileges are only available to those who adhere to the traditional societal norms. After section 377 was nullified, a lot of efforts have been made to legalize same-sex marriages but is it the ultimate solution to the problem at hand?

After half a decade of legalizing same-sex marriages, the discrimination against the L.G.B.T. community in America is heightened as now you are openly gay. In a nation like ours where reportedly most of the marriages are arranged and people are still facing a hard time in accepting inter-caste marriages, it wouldn't be a surprise if the same situation like that of America's is created. After all the freedom that comes with a choice, love and affection doesn't fit into the historically built structure of caste, class, colour, and religion.

Another one of the many issues that needs to be addressed is the patriarchal nature of marriage. The existing family structure in India requires family wealth to be passed on to generations. Hence, forcing people (particularly women) to marry someone they feel is 'right'. Our country has a religion-based social order. This views procreation as a necessity for the fulfilment of religious ceremonies such as marriage.

Moreover, to legalize same-sex marriages, laws governing marriage will have to be reframed to be gender-neutral. The legalization of same-sex marriage is portrayed as "redefining marriage" by many opponents. Laws like that of domestic violence and other laws on sexual harassment assume women to be a vulnerable party being exploited by the dominant. Therefore, changing their vocabulary to be gender-neutral could provide loopholes giving a chance to the perpetrator to victimize himself.

Indian society is a community-oriented society, where individualism is not supported in the least. Here, any representation of homosexuality is perceived as an effort to renounce tradition and encourage individualism. Hence, people view it as a menace to Indian society.

The right to marriage is a Human right. Indian Constitution has provided Article 21 within which the Right to Marry is a universal, but not fundamental right. Right to Marry is acknowledged at the global level, however, in India, there is no proper law for marriage rights. It is open to each person but the question remains unanswered. Whether it includes same-sex marriage?

It must be remembered that Indian society is patriarchal in nature and any person that has a different choice, which is not sanctioned by the 'order', scares them. As it is seen that legalizing homosexual marriage will destroy the idea of a traditional family and the holiness of marriage will succumb.

However, this shouldn't be a surprise when we say there is sufficient Hindu literature available that supports Homosexuality in Hinduism including same-sex marriages. Yes, it is true, Homosexuality has an old history in India. Everyone has heard about Ancient texts such as Rig Veda, right?

Even though these ancient texts date back almost 1500 BC, they contain sexual activities between women as signs of a feminine creation where sexuality was conditional on fertility and pleasure. In addition to that, various vestiges and sculptures represent these activities. Not only that, some historical testimonies of same-sex relationships are expressed in the Kamasutra, the persona of "Sikhandi" in Mahabharat, carvings of the temple at Khajuraho and much more.

But these events lost their importance with the arrival of Vedic Brahmanism, along with British Colonialism. Even though Manusmriti rendered severe punishments for women having a sexual relationship together, both sexual systems coincided, despite the variations in relative freedom and repression. Till British Colonialism destructed the concepts of homosexual expression.

Also, the British during the colonial era introduced 377 on the lines of The Buggery Act of 1533, passed during the reign of Henry VIII. It defined the unnatural sexual act as against the will of God. However, if we dig deeper into Indian history, we can find evidence of gender variance and non-heterosexuality in Hindu folk-lores and epics. Vishnu as Mohini (his only female avatar), procreated with Shiva to give birth to Lord Ayyappa. King Bhagiratha was born to two female parents, widowed Queens, whose birth was considered as a blessing and was socially accepted. Khajuraho temple in Madhya Pradesh, India famous for its architecture has displayed sculptures of sexual intercourse between the same sex.

Not only Hinduism, other religions such as Islam and Christianity also acknowledge homosexuality. Even if they traditionally acknowledge Homosexuality as a sin, one thing could be seen, that all the religions are admitting the fact that Homosexuality exists. This leads us to conclude that Homosexuality is not something unnatural. It could also be viewed in a way that balances nature and is natural.

In modern Indian society, sexuality is rarely discussed. But it should be taught and discussed from a primary level such as school. Legalising same-sex marriage has a long way to go, till then all efforts should be made to make Homosexuals feel comfortable and protected. Sex Education should be taught from the basic level of one's life. This way not only the LGBTQ+ community would feel protected and inclusive but also cis-gender people would know more about the community. Sex education would be a win-win situation for the people of India.

Crimes such as dowry, Sati, infanticides and child marriage are practices that stemmed from cultural dogma, but the Government yet took actions to stop them. The whole discussion of legalizing same-sex marriage is anything but a religious debate. One should understand the fact that Homosexuality is not a sin, but a way of pursuing happiness. Apart from irrational prejudice, no reason stops two gay people from getting married and enjoying the rights and protection which heterosexual couple take for granted. We are living in a world, which values a person's right to decide.

And homosexuality is neither something new nor is against India's culture. It always existed in our culture. So, why can't same-sex couples have the legitimacy to their life?

CHAPTER NINE

LEGALISING SEX WORK

Author: Kajal Arora, Advocate practising in Punjab Haryana High Court
Co-author: Komal Arora, Advocate practising in Punjab Haryana High Court

I did not bring this upon myself,
I had to escape the hell or I would lose myself.
I was 14 when I first felt the pain,
Today, this job leaves me everything to gain.
When he touched me, it felt so wrong,
And every time, I wondered for how long?
Open me up for the world to see
And still, I'll scream I'm free! I'm free! I'm free![i]

Sex work is normal work. It is a fact of life that we need to acknowledge and accept as the chances that it is going to fade away in nearfuture are grim. The origin of prostitution and sex work is as long as time. It is considered to be the oldest occupation in the world, yet it had a challenging and arduous journey. Unlike any other occupation which comes with its own labour rules and regulations, sex work was allowed to be tossed in open and it was left hanging in cold and dry with no regular benefits and protections. The debates surrounding sex work has been intermittent but to no avail. It never reached a consensus.

Let's consider all the germane factors weighing in debate of legalising sex work.

1. Question of consent

Sex work is not made a criminal activity in our law, but it is regulated by Immoral Trafficking Prevention Act, 1986. Women engaged in these actsare treated as 'victims' and those who exploitthem are 'perpetrators'. The problem is that this Act makes no distinction between consensual and non-consensual acts and equally punishes all.

Instead of punishing and attempting to take away source of livelihood from those consenting to sex work, the act should be focused only on non-consensual acts which due to denial of consent fall in the definition of rape under Section 375 IPC. Also, it needs to be made explicitly clear that not everyone in this occupation needs to be rescued. Some of these women voluntarily enter this profession and cannot be forced to quit and settle in shelter homes.

Legalising sex work will end the debate on legality of consensual acts.

2. Survival Sex prostitution

For some of these workers sex work is a mode of survival, a means to earn livelihood as the fact remains that it is business. It exists despite efforts to limit it.

It is a practice where women offer their bodies in return of basicnecessities like food, shelter. For them sex work is a way out of their homeless, deprived lives.Intimidating and coercing them out of their methods to survive doesn't seem to be an appropriate way to show our disapproval and objection to their occupation. Legalising sex work will license survival sex prostitution.

3. Labour rights

The rights and provisions for labour are concrete. It includes all rights of safe working conditions, fair income, reasonable working hours, right to protection against unemployment, freedom of association etc. As sex work is not legally recognised as legal work none of these rights are provided to these workers. That is an argument for legalising of sex work that they will be entitled to hygienic working conditions, protection from sexual violence and physical violence, right to be respected. In cases of violation they will be able to report it to police as if it is not recognised as legal work they are hesitant to approach the authorities which in return questions their choice of occupation and claim that they are not entitled to legal protection as what they do is an act not legally accepted. Legalising of sex work will allow workers to content against abrogation of their legal rights.

4. Social stigma

The ignominy of being attached to sex work makes it gruelling to assert thefundamental rights. The ostracization leads to mental stress and depression. Legalising sex work will enable them to receive psychological care and support.

5. Independence in occupation

For every person independence in occupation is important. It allows them to choose and select their course of employment. Choice gives meaning to profession. Similarly, sex workers should have option to decide their clients. Traditionally, the way sex work functions workers have nil bargaining powers. Legalising it will allow them to advertise their business and acquire medical histories of their clients. They will have the power to refuse sex work if client comes from history of sexual violence. Maintenance of records can be uncomplicated and straight forward.They can overtly enter into negotiations of their work with clients.

Spread of chronic infectious health diseases like AIDS in these workers is at risk as they are vulnerable and in no position to prevent these infections. Chances of acquiring and transmitting diseases during sex trade escalate as there is minimum societal, economic and legal factors to redeem their position.

<u>In addition to these considerations various organisations have come out to support sex work as legal work</u>

I. Universal declaration of human rights (UDHR)

The preamble simply provides that recognition of inherent dignity and equal and inalienable rights of all members of human family is foundation of freedom, justice and peace in this world.

Article 1 guarantees the right to dignity and equal rights whereas Article 23 gives us right to work without discrimination, get reasonable remuneration and to form unions.

II. Convention on elimination of all forms of discrimination against women (CEDAW)

The convention affirms that right to work is inalienable right. It provides choice of employment, access to work related benefits, occupational health and safetyprovisions.[ii]

III. International Labour organisation (ILO)

Ratification of recommendation 200 was widely appreciated as it is recognised as first step towards legalising sex work. ILO Decent work and 2030 agenda for sustainable development has four pillars as its agenda: employment creation, social protection, rights at work and social dialogue.[iii]Concept of decent work includes provision for fair income, productive opportunities and social protection.

IV. Human rights watch

In 2014, HRC gave its support to decriminalising of sex work. It even defined sex work as buying and selling of sexual acts including stripping, pornography, phone sex etc.[iv]

V. Budhadev karmaskar v. State of West Bengal[v]

In 2011 committee was appointed to advise and decide on issues of sex workers. But even after a decade the affair has not reached a consensus.The bench of J. Nageshwara Rao, J. A.S Bopanna and J. B.R Gavai critically examined that sex workers are not even treated as human beings and it is inhumane. The court directed UIDAI to issue aadhaar cards to sex workers without proof of residence. Also directions were given to police authorities to not abuse sex workers and to prohibit media from publishing their pictures during raid and rescue operations. The court noted that right to dignity is a fundamental right guaranteed to every citizen.

Bombay High court also held that prostitution is not an offence, adult woman has every right to choose her vocation.

In case of Manoj Shaw v State of west Bengal[vi]Calcutta High court held that sex workers should not be arrested, instead they are victims of crime.Before arrest notice under Section 41A crpc is a must. In another case Delhi High court sentenced accused to ten years imprisonment and gave a powerful judgment that occupation of victim is irrelevant to offence. Simply, because victim worked as sex worker doesn't confer any right to anyone to violate her dignity.

Some argue that illegality of occupation keeps demand and supply in check, it allows them to be not subjected to governmental regulations and may lead to loss of independence. But firm belief is that legalising sex work will allow government to regulate the profession and control the criminal elements like sexual violence, drug abuse, compulsory labour, exploitation. System should provide better working conditions for those who are engaged in voluntary sex work.

In the end we hope that the intense debate sparked with a slew of judgments of Apexcourt will unfold into protection of human rights of sex workers and will not be quenched easily without any final decision of government. Fingers crossed that unlike past time's damp squib this time these discussion will befructuous.

www.ingramcontent.com/pod-product-compliance
Lightning Source LLC
Chambersburg PA
CBHW072135150726

48002CB00004B/1520